Table of Contents

C
How To Use This Book
Introduction
Introduction: Going Further
Historical Highlights: The Genesis of Advance Directives
Historical Highlights: Going Further
Imagine the Unimaginable
Imagine the Unimaginable: Going Further
Some Serious Stuff
Some Serious Stuff: Going Further
Your Right to Your Own Future
Your Right to Your Own Future: Going Further
Know What You Want
Know What You Want: Going Further
Step 1: Plan Ahead
Step 1: Going Further
Step 2: Write It Down
Step 2: Going Further
Step 3: Whom Do You Trust?
Step 3: Going Further
Step 4: Phone a Friend
Step 4: Going Further
Step 5: Keep It Simple!
Step 5: Going Further

How To Use This Book

TAKING CARE AT THE END of Life: Five Steps to Writing a Meaningful and Practical Advance Directive is an easy-to-use book that will guide you through the process of designing and creating an advance directive. Such a document will help protect your interests and those of your loved ones in the case of dire medical circumstances that leave you incapable of making medical decisions on your own behalf.

The topic itself, that is, confronting our own mortality and ultimate demise, may be very upsetting. But if we avoid the many challenges involved in facing serious threats to our well-being, the unintended outcomes of emergency medical treatment may leave us with long-term or permanent loss of quality of life. In such a case a person may be unable to communicate in any meaningful way. A person may have lost the mental capacity to think for herself or himself. A person may be permanently dependent on others for the maintenance of his or her physical functioning.

On the other hand, having the foresight and taking the time and necessary steps to design and create an advance directive puts you in position to have control over how things go in a case in which you're unable to speak for yourself. Each chapter in **Taking Care at the End of Life** presents a specific component of the process of creating a clear and concise advance directive that accurately represents your preferences and desires regarding medical treatment in potential end-of-life circumstances.

Detailed instructions and links to online resources help streamline the activities and assist you in clarifying your thoughts, choosing a surrogate, and formalizing your advance directive.

Additionally, each chapter of **Taking Care at the End of Life** concludes with a Personal Reflection and a brief series of Action Steps to help facilitate and enrich the overall experience of creating this important and critical document. The peace of mind we obtain by helping protect our future in this way will provide immeasurable benefit to ourselves and our loved ones.

Remember — writing your advance directive is an affirmation of life. Let's get started!

Introduction

EVERYBODY NEEDS AN ADVANCE DIRECTIVE. Everyone needs the security such a document provides, whether you're a new college graduate or the oldest member of your retirement community. Advance directives help protect us, in dire medical circumstances, against unwanted medical procedures and the resultant loss of our life savings. Without an advance directive, our painstakingly accumulated financial resources could be drained all the way down to zero, and our family and friends would be unable to stop the process. Writing an advance directive is a smart and straightforward way to help protect our loved ones from such unwanted and devastating outcomes. To understand why an advance directive is important, we need to talk about some very difficult and potentially upsetting things.

Having an advance directive helps make sure your wishes, desires, and preferences are followed in case of a profound medical emergency. For example, you suffer a head trauma and are knocked unconscious. Or you have a health problem, possibly a serious one, and at a particular point in time you lose consciousness. You're discovered by a co-worker, friend, or family member, who calls 911. Emergency responders find you unconscious or possibly your heart has stopped. In the latter case CPR is performed, and after a few attempts your heart starts pumping and you open your eyes. Or your heart revives but you're unconscious and cannot eat or drink on your own, and the hospital team inserts a feeding tube and places you on a ventilator. Either way, if you've suffered significant brain damage and you eventually regain consciousness, you may no longer be the person you once were. You may have lost substantial capacity for taking care of yourself. You may not be able to understand what people are saying to you, and you may not be able to clearly articulate what it is you want.

Bottom line, your ability to function as an independent human being has been lost. But you're still alive. You may have clear thoughts inside your head, but you're unable to make your body do what you want it to do. Or you're conscious but you're unable to eat or drink on your own, and you permanently require artificial nutrition and hydration. You may not wish to live like that. Many people would deny this and say that life itself remains precious. That may be so and such a perspective is an individual prerogative. For those who would find such a set of circumstances onerous, for those who would wish to have a say in the matter and would choose otherwise, an advance directive is necessary to retain your freedom of choice. Your advance directive allows you to state your preferences and desires for how things will go when you're no longer able to speak on your own behalf.

What do I mean by this? In your advance directive, you have the opportunity to state which medical procedures will be acceptable and which will not be acceptable, in the case in which you are unable to state your preferences yourself. For example, you might state that the requirement for a feeding tube and/or a ventilator beyond 30 days is not acceptable and you would want them removed. Importantly, in your advance directive you specify who will speak on your behalf. Such a person is known as a **surrogate,** a person who has legal standing and represents your interests, in terms of medical treatment, when things have gone badly and you're unable to state your own preferences and desires. Your surrogate becomes your mouthpiece, in a sense. Your surrogate speaks for you and articulates what you would want done and what you do not want done.

No one wants to consider these things. It's painful and possibly frightening to imagine such circumstances and put your thoughts down on paper in this way. But if we don't think about what might happen, if we don't plan ahead and the worst does happen, we're stuck. We're at the mercy of those who would take care of us, such as hospital medical staff. Medical professionals want to help; they're trained to saves lives. But those medical professionals don't know what we ourselves would prefer. If, having suffered a devastating injury or severe, potentially terminal illness, we would no longer wish to continue living but have not made our desires and preferences expressly known, the medical **standard of care** will be imposed.

That standard of care is to save your life, regardless of the cost to you and your family and regardless of your loss of quality of life as you'd wish to live it. With all the best intentions, your medical providers may be condemning you to a lifetime of severe disability or otherwise severely compromised quality of life. And, profound financial demands will be placed on you and your dependents. If this doesn't sound like what you would want, it's time to sit down and write your advance directive.

Introduction: Going Further

Personal Reflection

What thoughts, issues, and conflicts are raised by the prospect of writing an advance directive? What are the implications for your notions and concepts about the meaning and value of life? What does the concept "quality of life" mean to you? What are the most important things in your life right now?

Action Steps

1. Make a list of five family members and/or friends you speak to most frequently.
2. Make a list of five capabilities or activities that are important to you (for example, reading, bike riding, quilting).
3. Write a paragraph or two describing how these people and activities contribute to your quality of life.

Historical Highlights: The Genesis of Advance Directives

ADVANCE DIRECTIVES (ALSO KNOWN AS living wills) are a relatively new development in how we think about our interactions with doctors and hospitals. In the old days, physicians were trusted advisers who could be counted on to make decisions with our best interests in mind and to do the right thing. Unfortunately, in certain circumstances neither of these notions is still valid. In critical end-of-life situations, if you have lost the cognitive ability to make your own decisions, what may be done to you in a hospital in the name of saving your life may have nothing at all to do with what you would have wanted for yourself.

Physicians, nurses, and medical staff are trained to keep the patient alive. Further, there is a legal presumption that a patient would wish measures to be taken to save his or her life. The quality of life that is the outcome of these life-preserving procedures is not a consideration. The person may be left with a permanent requirement for a feeding tube (artificial nutrition and hydration), a breathing machine (a ventilator), or both. The person may be left with a permanent loss of cognitive capacity and may never again be able to talk with family and friends, never again be able to understand what's being said, or never again be able to even recognize loved ones. An even more extreme result of medical intervention to save the person's life is a persistent vegetative state, in which the patient is permanently unaware of self and environment.

Thus, the need for an advance directive is the direct result of modern developments in medical technology. Now, these technological advances came about as a result of the desire to save more lives, and many people have greatly benefited from CPR (cardiopulmonary resuscitation), feeding tubes, and ventilators. But the formidable problem in using such techniques and devices is that the ultimate outcome is unknown. Medical and emergency personnel can never predict how well the patient is going to function once he or she is brought back from the brink of death. Some patients will do well and thrive, possibly with minor or moderate but acceptable limitations and deficits. But others will be severely, permanently impaired. Many people, given the choice, would not wish to "live like a vegetable". Many people would not wish to live a life in which they have substantially lost awareness of themselves and their environment. Many people would not wish to continue an existence in which they could not, in some form or another, read a book or interact, in any way at all, with family and friends. Many people would choose not to undergo live-saving measures if the outcome would be severe loss of quality of life.

But no one can know in advance what the outcome will be. As medical technology is omnipresent, at least in urban areas, it becomes important to provide ourselves with a defense against unwanted, unasked-for medical interventions. Technology in the medical case, as in all others, is a mixed blessing. Such technology is good for some, but not good at all for others.

Karen Ann Quinlan

This dichotomy became very apparent, for the first time, in the case of Karen Ann Quinlan. On the night of April 15th, 1975, Ms. Quinlan ceased breathing for two 15-minute periods. The cause of her cessation of respiration is unclear. She was taken to a local New Jersey hospital where an examination showed that her pupils were nonreactive and she was unresponsive, even to deep pain. Several days later a follow-up examination found her comatose with evidence of loss of cortical (higher brain) function. Ultimately, Karen's condition progressed to that of a persistent vegetative state. She was maintained on a respirator, required artificial nutrition and hydration, and was supported by 24-hour nursing assistance.

Ultimately, Joseph Quinlan, Karen's father, petitioned the court to be appointed his daughter's guardian. As her guardian, her father planned to authorize the discontinuance of all extraordinary medical procedures that were sustaining Karen's life. The Supreme Court of New Jersey declared that "no external compelling state interest could compel Karen to endure the unendurable". [*In re Quinlan*, 70 N.J. 10 (1976), 355 A. 2d 647] The court ruled that Joseph Quinlan had the right to choose an attending physician. If the responsible attending physician determined that there was no reasonable possibility of Karen's returning to a cognitive, self-aware state, and that life-sustaining treatment should be discontinued, then upon agreement of the hospital Ethics Committee, the present life-support procedures and equipment could be withdrawn. The mechanical ventilator was discontinued. Subsequently, Karen survived in a persistent vegetative state for almost an additional 10 years and died in 1985.

Nancy Cruzan

A second landmark case involved Nancy Cruzan, a resident of the State of Missouri. In January 1983, 25-year-old Ms. Cruzan lost control of her car, was flung from her vehicle, and landed face-down in a water-filled ditch. Paramedics resuscitated her, even though they found no vital signs. Nancy was in a coma for 3 weeks and then was diagnosed as being in a persistent vegetative state. Her parents wanted life support to be withdrawn, but the Missouri state hospital opposed their request. A trial court found that evidence of a conversation Nancy had had with a friend, in which she stated she would not want to live in a vegetative state, was sufficient to permit termination of artificial nutrition and hydration.

But the Supreme Court of Missouri overturned the trial court's decision, ruling that such a conversation was insufficient. The court ruled that no person can assume a choice for an incompetent patient (one who has lost cognitive capacity) in the absence of documentation required by the Missouri Living Will statute or clear and convincing evidence required to prove a patient's intentions. A casual discussion with a roommate was deemed insufficient to meet the clear and convincing evidence standard. Further, the Missouri Supreme Court ruled that the Missouri guardianship statute did not provide authority for Nancy's parents to authorize termination of her nutrition and hydration support. The problem, of course, was that Nancy had not executed an advance directive/living will, nor had she appointed a surrogate to make decisions on her behalf.

The Cruzans appealed the Missouri Supreme Court decision to the U.S. Supreme Court. The U.S. Supreme Court ruled that Missouri has the right to apply a clear and convincing evidence standard in such a case. The State may "simply assert an unqualified interest in the preservation of human life to be weighed against the constitutionally protected interests of the individual". [*Cruzan v. Director, Missouri Department of Health*, 497 U.S. 261 (1990)] Missouri recognizes that a surrogate may act for an incompetent patient, but requires that withdrawal of treatment be proved by clear and convincing evidence.

In her concurrence, Justice Sandra Day O'Connor narrowed her interpretation of this decision. She noted that few individuals provide "explicit oral or written instructions regarding their intent to refuse medical treatment should they become incompetent". Justice O'Connor stated that the instructions regarding medical treatment of a surrogate decision-maker may be constitutionally protected in the sense of upholding a patient's liberty interest under the Due Process Clause of the Fourteenth Amendment. She indicated that a future court determination may rule that the Constitution requires the States to implement the decisions of a patient's duly appointed surrogate.

In the event, the Cruzans took their case back to the Missouri courts, having identified additional witnesses testifying to Nancy's wishes and desires regarding end-of-life circumstances. In December 1990, clear and convincing evidence was established and removal of the feeding tube was permitted. Twelve days later Nancy Cruzan died, eight years after the auto crash that left her in a persistent vegetative state.

Importantly, *Cruzan v. Director, MDH* affirmed that "a competent person has a constitutionally protected liberty interest in refusing unwanted medical treatment", including a constitutionally protected right to refuse lifesaving nutrition and hydration. The problem immediately arises of how to protect the rights of a person who is not competent to make medical decisions. The U.S. Supreme Court expressly stated in *Cruzan* that a competent person's constitutionally protected right to refuse life-saving treatment "does not mean that an incompetent person should possess the same right, since such a person is unable to make an informed and voluntary choice to exercise that hypothetical right or any other right". Thus, we can conclude that additional rights and safeguards of those rights are required.

Terri Schiavo

Terri Schiavo collapsed in her home on February 25th, 1990, having suffered cardiac arrest as a result of a potassium imbalance. She was in a coma for several months, and subsequently emerged with a sleep-wake cycle, that is, her eyes would open following a sleep period. But she did not demonstrate any evidence of self-awareness or awareness of her environment. In other words, Ms. Schiavo's cardiac arrest resulted in a persistent vegetative state. She never regained consciousness.

After several years of attempts at various treatments, Michael Schiavo, Terri's husband, began to understand that her condition was irreversible and he began to assert that his wife would not have wanted to be kept alive in a persistent vegetative state. In contrast, Terri's parents insisted that their daughter be continued on life-sustaining treatment, i.e., artificial hydration and nutrition. Michael Schiavo took the matter to a Florida trial court (Sixth Circuit Court of Florida). The trial court found in 2000 that credible witnesses had presenting clear and convincing evidence that Terri would not want to continue living in a condition such as that of a persistent vegetative state. But Terri's parents, Robert and Mary Schindler, appealed the trial court's ruling permitting the withdrawal of the feeding tube that was keeping their daughter alive.

As the case progressed through the courts, the Schindlers maintained that new treatments might restore cognitive function to their daughter. They believed that Terri responded to them. A videotape was made public in which Terri appears to be smiling and moaning in response to her mother's voice and appears to follow a balloon with her eyes. But the eyes of a person in a persistent vegetative state may move about when the person is awake. The person may breathe, open her mouth, and yawn. However, in a persistent vegetative state there is no evidence of awareness of self or environment, no meaningful response to stimuli, and no receptive or expressive language. [American Academy of Neurology: Practice parameters, assessment, and management of patients in the persistent vegetative state. Neurology 45:1015-1018, 1995] Despite the presence of reflex behaviors that give the appearance of conscious interaction to those who hold onto hope for a miraculous recovery, restoration of consciousness after 3 months is rare in adults with persistent vegetative state as a consequence of nontraumatic injury. [The Multi-Society Task Force on PVS: Medical aspects of the persistent vegetative state. Part 2. N Engl J Med 330:1572-1579, 1994] By the early 2000s, Terri Schiavo had been in a persistent vegetative state for more than 10 years. Recovery was not possible.

The Florida 2nd District Court of Appeals upheld the trial court's decision. Subsequently, the Terri Schiavo case played out in public view. An attempt was made to bring the case to the Florida Supreme Court, but the court declined to review the decision of the 2nd District Court of Appeals. Then redress was sought via the Florida state legislature. The legislature obliged and on October 21, 2003 passed 2003-418, "Act for the Relief of the Parents of Theresa Marie Schiavo" ("Terri's Law"). The law gave Governor Jeb Bush the authority "to issue a one-time stay to prevent the withholding of nutrition and hydration from a patient" based on a set of criteria that applied specifically to Terri Schiavo's circumstances. The PEG (percutaneous endoscopic gastrostomy) tube was reinserted, but a year later the Florida Supreme Court declared 2003-418 unconstitutional, as it violated the separation of powers.

Following refusal by the U.S. Supreme Court to hear an appeal, Judge George W. Greer (the trial court judge) ordered that the PEG tube be withdrawn on March 18, 2005. Next, the U.S. Congress passed a bill titled "For the relief of the parents of Theresa Marie Schiavo" which was signed by President George W. Bush on March 21, 2005. This act provided that a Florida U.S. District Court would hear a suit based on the "alleged violation of any right of Theresa Marie Schiavo" relating to withholding or withdrawal of life-saving treatment. But the U.S. District Court denied the request for a temporary restraining order, stating a substantial likelihood of success on the merits of the claims had not been demonstrated. Terri Schiavo died on March 31, 2005.

One of the many conclusions that may be drawn from these three compelling, tragic cases is the importance of having an advance directive in place. Karen Quinlan, Nancy Cruzan, and Terri Schiavo each lived for many years in a persistent vegetative state. In each case extensive time, effort, and resources were expended in attempts to obtain appropriate court decisions.

State supreme courts were involved in the Quinlan and Cruzan cases and a district court of appeals was involved in the Schiavo case, as well as a state legislature and the U.S. Congress. The existence of a notarized advance directive, one that clearly stated the patient's preferences and desires concerning end-of-life circumstances and designated a person or persons to act as the patient's surrogate, would have facilitated much more prompt resolution of each of these cases. Such a document would have provided answers to questions regarding clear and convincing evidence, questions such as those raised in Missouri as well as Florida. Interested parties might choose to challenge a decision to terminate life support, but the existence of an appropriately formatted advance directive would likely trump such attempts to interfere with a person's wishes regarding decision-making at the end of life.

The question for each of us concerns a willingness to set aside time to draw up a few documents and to consider potentially difficult and possibly deeply upsetting issues and circumstances. Each of us must inquire whether we're willing to take some modest actions on our own behalf, actions that would greatly ease the burdens on ourselves and our loved ones if the unthinkable comes to pass. Putting the matter simply, if we fail to take actions such as preparing an advance directive and if the worst happens, then our future welfare and well-being will be at the mercy of the court system. Our life savings and all our assets may be swept away in an unending sea of hospital and long-term care expenses. Awareness of these possibilities will likely cause reasonably prudent people to take the necessary actions, specifically, to draw up an advance directive, have it notarized, and inform selected friends and loved ones about the existence of such a document. In the following chapters, we're going to learn how to design and create a suitable advance directive.

Historical Highlights: Going Further

Personal Reflection

What does the Supreme Court's statement in *Cruzan v. Director, MDH* that "a competent person has a constitutionally protected liberty interest in refusing unwanted medical treatment" mean for you? In what types of situations might you choose to refuse medical treatment? What concerns might you have about the use of life-saving treatment?

Action Steps

1. Read the summary of the *Cruzan* decision.
2. Write a paragraph or two discussing how the rights of patients and the personal interests of family members might conflict.
3. Follow-up by writing a paragraph or two describing how such potential conflicts might be resolved.

Imagine the Unimaginable

WE'RE NOW GOING TO TALK about some very hard things. I want you to imagine the unimaginable. (Not that this is going to happen to you.) Just imagine some person, living a happy life, essentially minding his or her own business. Something happens. For example, the person might suffer a stroke (a cardiovascular accident) and be rendered unconscious. The person's spouse or partner finds their loved one prostrate, not responding, and calls 911. The emergency medical technicians (EMTs) arrive and the person is transported to the hospital, where numerous tests are done. The person is placed on artificial hydration and nutrition and everybody waits. The patient (the formerly independent person has become a "patient") is essentially asleep. An MRI study shows there has been substantial bleeding into the brain. Importantly, no one knows what the person will be like when she wakes up. Will she have full capacity? In other words, will she be able not only to think for herself, but will she be able to express herself clearly? Will she be able to state what she'd like done? Will she be able to make medical care decisions for herself? Will she be capable of understanding what is being said to her and be able to say what she wants to say? Additionally, will she be able to move her body purposefully? Will she be able to eat and drink on her own? Will she be able to walk around? Will she be able to read and watch TV? In other words, will she be the same person she was before she had her illness?

The main problem facing patients and families is that, in such dire medical circumstances, everything we take for granted in terms of our functioning and capabilities as human beings is overturned. Even our most basic activities require incredible neurologic complexity. A person may wake up from a period of unconsciousness, and this could be a joyful outcome. But the person may now be incapable of feeding himself, attending to physical needs, reading, writing, or any cognitive comprehension. Many people, if they had the choice, might elect to avoid such a possible scenario by stating in advance their desire not to be resuscitated.

Imagine another very difficult situation. A young person is driving his car and is hit head-on by a drunk driver. The young person had neglected to fasten his seatbelt and is launched through the windshield by the collision. Remarkably, he is alive when the EMTs and police arrive. He is breathing on his own, but he is unconscious. Artificial hydration and nutrition is started at the hospital. Weeks go by and the patient remains unconscious. In this case, MRI has shown some bleeding into the brain, but the patient also has a **contrecoup** injury. His brain has been injured by banging into the bones on the opposite side of his skull. The patient may never wake up. If he does, it is unknown what capabilities will be retained. Remarkably, after several more months he does open his eyes. But it is demonstrated that he is unaware of his environment and unaware of himself. Essentially, he goes through sleep and wake cycles, but he is not conscious. He is in a vegetative state and after 30 days he is declared to be in a persistent vegetative state.

It's useful to distinguish between being conscious, being in a coma, and being in a persistent vegetative state. A person who is *conscious* demonstrates wakefulness (level of consciousness) and awareness (content of consciousness). [Laureys S, et al: Coma. In *Encyclopedia of Neuroscience*, Volume 2. New York, Academic Press, 2009, pp 1133-1142] Thus, a person in a *coma* is unconscious, as such a person is neither awake nor aware. A person in a persistent vegetative state may be awake at times, but he is not aware of self or environment, and such a person is also characterized as being unconscious. The distinguishing feature between coma and persistent vegetative state is that, in a persistent vegetative state, the person is awake. As the Multi-Society Task Force on PVS stated in 1994, "Awareness requires wakefulness, but wakefulness can be present without awareness." [MSTF on PVS: Medical aspects of the persistent vegetative state. NEJM 330(21):1499-1508, 1994]

The term "persistent vegetative state" was first used in 1972 to describe the condition of severely brain-damaged patients in whom coma has progressed to a state of wakefulness in the absence of detectable awareness. [Jennett B, Plum F: Persistent vegetative state after brain damage: a syndrome in search of a name. Lancet 1:734-737, 1972] The clinical criteria for the diagnosis of persistent vegetative state were established in 1990 by the AMA Council on Scientific Affairs and the Council on Ethical and Judicial Affairs. A persistent vegetative state is characterized by complete lack of awareness of the self and environment, accompanied by sleep-wake cycles. There is either partial or complete preservation of brainstem functioning. The person can breathe on her own and does not require respiratory support. But artificial nutrition and hydration is required as the person is unconscious, even though, in a wake cycle, her eye's are open. The Quality Standards Subcommittee [QSS] of the American Academy of Neurology published further definitions to clarify a diagnosis of persistent vegetative state. [The Quality Standards Subcommittee of the American Academy of Neurology: Practice parameters: assessment and management of patients in the persistent vegetative state (summary statement). Neurology 45(5):1015-1018, 1995] The QSS stated that a vegetative state can be defined as being persistent at 1 month. Persistent vegetative state can be judged permanent 12 months after traumatic injury and after 3 months in nontraumatic injury. The QSS states that criteria for diagnosis of persistent vegetative state include no evidence of purposeful or voluntary responses to visual, auditory, or tactile stimuli and no evidence of language comprehension or expression.

Regarding the possibility of being maintained in a persistent vegetative state (PVS), a 2003 study concluded that a substantial majority of people "would choose (prospectively) to reject life-sustaining treatment in a PVS if the operative assumption were that they would never recover consciousness". [Mappes TA: Persistent vegetative state, prospective thinking, and advance directives. Kennedy Institute of Ethics Journal 13(2):119-139, 2003] Of course, critical information is required to assist one in making an informed prospective choice, that is, when one is crafting an advance directive. The Multi-Society Task Force on PVS indicates that for adult patients in a persistent vegetative state for 3 months following a traumatic brain injury, the probability of achieving moderate disability or making a good recovery at 12 months was 16%. The MSTF notes that patients with moderate disability are independent and can resume almost all activities of daily living. In contrast, for adult patients in a PVS for 3 months after a nontraumatic brain injury (for example, as a result of stroke, heart attack, diabetic coma, or drowning), the probability of achieving moderate disability or making a good recovery at 12 months was 1%. For adult patients who had suffered a traumatic injury and were in a persistent vegetative state for 6 months, only 4% were anticipated to achieve moderate disability or make a good recovery at 12 months. Zero percent of adult patients in a PVS for 6 months after a nontraumatic injury were expected to achieve moderate disability or make a good recovery at 12 months. [Multi-Society Task Force on PVS on PVS: Medical aspects of the persistent vegetative state. Part 2. NEJM 330(22):1572-1579, 1994] These data can also be viewed from the perspective of incidence, that is, actual outcomes, in contrast to probabilities. Of 434 patients in a PVS 1 month following a traumatic injury, 17% achieved moderate disability at 12 months and 7% achieved good recovery at 12 months. Of 169 patients in a PVS 1 month following a nontraumatic injury, only 3% achieved moderate disability at 12 months and only 1% achieved good recovery at 12 months.

Our key task is to assess these data in the best way possible to assist us in crafting an advance directive that represents what we want to have happen in specific circumstances. The Multi-Society Task Force found that for those in a persistent vegetative state 3 months following a traumatic brain injury, the likelihood of achieving a moderate or good recovery at 12 months is 16%. Each of us needs to consider whether such odds are worth pursuing. In contrast, for those in a persistent vegetative state 3 months following a nontraumatic brain injury, the likelihood of achieving a moderate or good recovery at 12 months is 1%. These odds are considerably longer. Also, for those in a persistent vegetative state 6 months following a traumatic brain injury, the likelihood of achieving a moderate or good recovery at 12 months is 4%. For those in a persistent vegetative state 6 months following a nontraumatic brain injury, the likelihood of achieving a moderate or good recovery at 12 months is 0%. Thus at 3 months following a traumatic brain injury, some people might assess a 16% chance of a moderate or good recovery at 12 months to be acceptable. Such a person might state in her advance directive that she does not wish to be maintained on life-sustaining treatment if she continues to be in a persistent vegetative state 6 months following a traumatic brain injury. Others would assess the same 16% chance as unacceptable. Those individuals could state in their advance directives that they do not wish to be maintained on life-sustaining treatment beyond 3 months following a traumatic brain injury. In scenarios involving a persistent vegetative state following a nontraumatic brain injury, such as in a stroke, heart attack, or diabetic coma, the likelihood of a moderate or good recovery is considerably poorer. Your advance directive could state that you do not wish to be maintained on life-sustaining treatment if you continue to be in a persistent vegetative state 3 months following a nontraumatic brain injury.

Ultimately, of course, it is not possible for us to account for every scenario or clinical circumstance. But by including a few specific statements in our advance directive regarding two or three possible situations, we have empowered our surrogate to take appropriate action on our behalf. Our surrogate will take such appropriate action in consideration of our stated preferences and in the context of the actual clinical circumstances, that is, what has actually happened to us (the medical history) and our current situation (the diagnosis, test results, and anticipated outcome).

Returning to our discussion of the young car-crash victim in a persistent vegetative state, his family is dismayed, to say the least. It doesn't appear as if he will ever recover, but his body continues to function. The choices are terrible on all sides. Naturally, as the patient was a young person, he never considered that anything like this could ever happen. People in their 20s do not consider end-of-life circumstances. It's almost unnatural to do so. But the lack of such planning has placed his life and his family's well-being in a precarious situation. As we'll discuss in <u>Step 3: Whom Do You Trust?</u>, in the absence of an advance directive the possibility exists for the application of either **substituted judgment** or **best interests**. But in the current scenario, as the patient had never made any statement about what to do if he were ever in such circumstances, everyone's options are limited. Had he sat down for an hour and composed an advance directive, the entire situation would be much different. The advance directive provides guidance. With an advance directive there is a legal framework from which to proceed. In the absence of an advance directive, all that's possible is ongoing tragedy.

Imagine the Unimaginable: Going Further

Personal Reflection

What value might there be in the willingness to consider a personal scenario such as being in a persistent vegetative state? Given that the future is unknown and unpredictable, how might you attempt to safeguard your family's well-being?

Action Steps

1. Write a paragraph or two discussing the meaning of "quality of life".
2. Write a paragraph or two describing what constitutes an acceptable quality of life.
3. Write a paragraph or two describing circumstances that would constitute an unacceptable quality of life.

Some Serious Stuff

    THINK ABOUT THIS. IT'S 10:30AM on Monday morning. You've left your office and are on your way to an early lunch meeting with a client. You're driving south on the local interstate, listening to National Public Radio, and ruminating about what kind of savings you're going to need to send your two kids to college. You're doing 70 in the left-hand lane, nothing unusual, traffic is moving nicely, there's plenty of space between you and the SUV in front of you. Then, from out of nowhere, an oncoming car veers across the northbound lanes and jumps the median directly in front of you. Your car slams into the unavoidable obstruction. Your torso jackknifes forward and your forehead violently impacts the steering wheel. Dazed and woozy, you manage to guide your ruined car to a skidding stop on the righthand shoulder. The last thing you remember is trying to unbuckle your seatbelt. Two weeks later you wake up and find yourself in a bed in a hospital room.

    Or consider this. You and your wife have just arrived home from a dinner party celebrating her 65th birthday. It's 11:45PM on a Friday evening in late June. A chorus of crickets are chirping at full volume beyond the margins of your patio. A nightingale sings his lovely, eerie melody in the near distance. As you get ready for bed, you think about your great good fortune in having met this wonderful woman, your partner and life companion, on that lucky day more than 30 years ago. A few minutes later, you're both situated comfortably under the light summer covers. Your wife snuggles closer and you wrap your arm around her as you drift off to sleep. But the next morning when your wife wakes up, she's surprised to find you're still in bed, apparently asleep beside her. "Hey, lazy bones," she chuckles, giving you a gentle shove. "Aren't you going to the gym?" Expecting but not receiving a sarcastic response, she leans over and kisses you on the cheek, whispering, "Wake up." Concerned now, as such ministrations are usually effective, she shakes you harder, and then harder still. Then she snatches her phone from the nightstand and calls 911. Five days go by before your eyes open and your gaze sweeps uncomprehendingly across the unfamiliar surround of your local hospital's stroke unit.

Both scenarios are horrific and both happen all the time. The details vary, but the circumstances are identical. A previously healthy and well person is now far from well. In fact, the person is so far from well that he or she cannot communicate their wishes, desires, and preferences for what they want done in terms of medical care. In our two hypothetical cases both patients, the 35-year-old and the 70-year old, are conscious. Each one has woken up. Their eyes are open, they respond to stimuli, and they are aware of their environment. But, at present, neither one can communicate. Neither one demonstrates the ability to understand verbal or written instructions or queries and neither one can speak clearly or write legibly. Speech is nothing more than garbled syllables. Attempts at writing produce meaningless scrawls. As a result of these losses, temporary or otherwise, each person has lost the capacity to make health care decisions on his or her own behalf. Each person, at present, requires another to make such decisions for them. The issues we're describing involve the concepts of competence and capacity.

Competence refers to decision-making capability. But the nature of the choice needs to be specified, as well as the conditions under which it is to be made. [Buchanan A, Brock DW: Deciding for Others: Competency. Millbank Q 64(2):67-80, 1986] For example, a post-stroke patient or a patient with a traumatic brain injury may be able to point to his or her preference for breakfast when shown a picture of scrambled eggs and a picture of oatmeal. The patient is competent to make that decision. But when asked whether they desire medication to help ensure a good night's sleep, neither patient is able to respond appropriately. Neither patient is competent to make such a medical decision. Thus, patients may be capable of making choices that do not require higher levels of reasoning, such as those involving food or clothing or even whether they wish to watch TV or page through an illustrated book. But choices involving higher cognitive functions, such as the ability to follow a chain of reasoning, are not possible. Competence is decision-relative and the context needs to be specified. The question becomes, "Does the patient have the capacity to perform a particular decision-making task, at a particular time and under specified conditions?"

Medical staff are therefore required to assess a patient's capacity to perform medical decision-making. Such capacity is evaluated based on four key criteria:

- The ability to understand risks and benefits
- The ability to apply risks and benefits to one's own situation
- The ability to make a reasoned decision consistent with one's beliefs and values
- The ability to express a preference and communicate that decision

All criteria must be fulfilled in rendering an assessment that a person has the capacity to make medical decisions on his or her own behalf, that is, to accept or refuse a particular medical procedure or service. These criteria are necessarily rigorous as they are intended to fulfill two complementary goals, those of (1) protecting and promoting the patient's health and well-being and (2) respecting the patient's right of self-determination.

For example, following either a stroke or a traumatic brain injury, medical staff may recommend drainage of an intracranial hemorrhage or other fluid accumulation. There may be substantial risks associated with such a procedure and significant risks related to taking no action. One patient may not be able to understand the risks and benefits. Another patient may not be able to express a preference. A third may state she doesn't want the procedure, but this appears inconsistent with the patient's well-known long-term plans for caring for her grandchildren, and she is unable to effectively explain her choice. In all cases the patient has not fulfilled the criteria required for a determination of capacity. Other parties will then make such a decision on behalf of the patient. Each of us must ask, "Who do I want making these decisions?" Do I want a team of doctors or hospital administrators, none of whom knows me, to make life-or-death decisions for me? Or do I want a family member, good friend, or other loved one on my side to make difficult choices on my behalf if I'm not capable of doing so? If we want someone we know, someone who cares about us on a close, personal level, to help us in such a critical time of need, we must make plans in advance. We must, in advance, designate a surrogate to make decisions for us when we're not capable of making those decisions.

Some Serious Stuff: Going Further

Personal Reflection

Sit quietly for 10 minutes and consider all the blessings (the value, the benefits, the relationships, the experiences) you derive from being alive, healthy, and well. Next, consider what it might be like to lose the capability of interacting meaningfully with all these aspects of your life.

Action Steps

1. Create a "Top Five List of Unfinished Business".
2. Choose one item on this list and write a paragraph describing how you will complete this task and be able to cross it off your list.
3. Imagine you have completed this task, project, or personal matter. Write a paragraph describing the benefits you and others derive from this completion.

Your Right to Your Own Future

THE U.S. SUPREME COURT LONG ago affirmed the principle of patient autonomy, that is, the patient's right to choose or refuse medical treatment. In the frequently cited case, *Schloendorff v. Society of New York Hospital* [105 NE 92, 93 (N.Y. 1914)], Justice Benjamin Cardozo wrote, "Every human being of adult years and sound mind has a right to determine what shall be done with his own body." This landmark ruling enshrined the right of individual decision-making with respect to health care. But the need for legal guidelines regarding medical decision-making on behalf of a patient not of "sound mind" was not a consideration in the early part of the 20th century. Life-and-death decisions were much more straightforward 100 years ago. It was a matter of course that a legal guardian would support life-saving medical procedures on behalf of a patient who was not of sound mind, that is, one who lacked capacity.

But there was no cardiopulmonary resuscitation back then. There was no technology to provide artificial nutrition and hydration. These methods and tools for prolonging life had not been developed or invented as yet, and there was no notion of extending life beyond the body's own natural stopping point. The problem we face, in the early part of the 21st century, is that the indiscriminate application of such life-preserving procedures is nothing better than a roll of the dice with respect to predicting the capabilities and level of consciousness of the person whose life has been brought back from the brink. You might go to sleep one night, in the comfort of your home, fully in command of all your faculties and gifts as a human being, and return to a semblance of consciousness 48 hours later, bereft of all your higher cognitive functions and unable to care for any of your bodily processes. In the worst case, you will never regain any of your lost abilities and will persist in such a state for months, years, or even more than a decade. This minimal level of existence, this highly compromised quality of life, has been thrust upon you by medical professionals whose sole criterion is to preserve life at any cost. Justice Cardozo, writing in 1914, did not account for the circumstance in which a person, no longer of sound mind, might wish to refuse medical procedures such as life-sustaining treatment, if only he or she were capable of doing so. Herein lies the necessity for writing your advance directive.

The cases of Karen Ann Quinlan, Nancy Cruzan, and Terri Schiavo all emphasize the need for protecting your rights and interests in the case in which you are no longer able to speak for yourself. But special requirements may inhere in the process of safeguarding these rights. In *Cruzan v. Director, Missouri Department of Health* (1990), the U.S. Supreme Court affirmed that states have the right to "simply assert an unqualified interest in the preservation of human life to be weighed against the constitutionally protected interests of the individual". At issue was the means of expression and the aptness of such expression of the constitutionally protected interests ("rights") of an individual not of "sound mind". As states retain an unqualified interest in the preservation of human life, a state may appropriately require stringent evidence supporting a choice to terminate such life. In *Cruzan*, the State of Missouri required "clear and convincing evidence" that Nancy Cruzan would not want her life to be preserved in a persistent vegetative state. Ultimately, clear and convincing evidence was established and removal of a feeding tube was permitted. But Nancy Cruzan had had to persist in a vegetative state for 8 years until the courts resolved her status and she was legally allowed to die.

Thus, based on the 1914 *Schloendorff* decision, you have the right to refuse cardiopulmonary resuscitation and artificial nutrition and hydration. Your advance directive formalizes these preferences at a time when you are of sound mind. Additionally many jurisdictions, including New York State and the State of California, have enshrined the right to appoint a surrogate to make medical decisions on your behalf when you are not of sound mind, and your advance directive embodies this right. But it's important to recognize that casual conversation with a friend or even a spouse regarding your desire not to live "like a vegetable" may fail the clear and convincing evidence test in many jurisdictions. Hospital ethics committees themselves may find such assertions on the part of well-meaning family members and friends insufficient to withhold or withdraw life-sustaining treatment. If you are concerned regarding the possibility of your life being prolonged by medical treatment in circumstances which you would find unacceptable, you must formalize your preferences and wishes in an advance directive. A lucid, consistent document, whose existence is known by a family member and/or close friend, will help fulfill a clear and convincing evidence standard.

In *Cruzan*, Justice Harry Blackmun wrote, "It is unrealistic to say that the preservation of life is an absolute, without regard to the quality of life. . . . It is appropriate to consider the quality of life in making decisions about the extraordinary medical treatment." Emergency responders usually do not know how long a person has been unconscious or for how long his or her heart has stopped. Without instructions to the contrary, these well-meaning professionals will attempt to restore a heartbeat or attempt to ensure you are receiving proper nutrition to maintain life if you are unconscious. But such good intentions may have quite negative outcomes, in the case in which the person whose life has been "saved" wakes up to an unacceptably diminished quality of life. Advance directives were designed to counter such possibilities and to ensure the ability to assert the "negative" right to refuse medical care.

Sitting in the comfort of one's home, facing a computer screen or reading on a portable device, such scenarios may seem far-fetched or unlikely. But the purpose of an advance directive is to guard against the worst. You have the right to declare your preferences regarding refusal of medical treatment in an emergency situation, in an end-of-life situation, or otherwise. You have the right to refuse treatment, regardless of the nature of the outcome. If you would not wish to continue living if being alive required being attached to tubes and machines 24 hours a day for months or years, then it's critically important to memorialize your wishes in an advance directive. Based on the principle of patient autonomy, that is, your right to choose or refuse treatment, medical providers are required to honor your stated wishes, even in a life-or-death circumstance. They may try to persuade your family to institute treatment or maintain current treatment. But your surrogate is empowered to uphold your desires and to make sure your rights are observed, provided you have documented clear and convincing evidence of your wishes.

Again, it's important to consider these things when we are well. We never know what's going to happen. By creating an advance directive, if the worst does occur, you have protected your future and, by implication, the future of your loved ones. An advance directive is your best protection against uncertainty. Without formal documentation of your wishes and preferences, your friends and loved ones will have to expend great quantities of time and energy to try to ensure that you live or die on your own terms. Memorializing your preferences in an advance directive is the best strategy for all concerned.

Your Right to Your Own Future: Going Further

Personal Reflection

Consider that your rights as an individual may not be permanent. For example, if a democratic government is defeated in war, the rights of its former citizens are swept away. Even in a democratic society various rights are transient, depending on contemporary legislation and the actions of the courts. For you, what are your most important rights?

Action Steps

The American Declaration of Independence states that all men "are endowed by their Creator with certain unalienable Rights, that among these are Life, Liberty and the pursuit of Happiness".

1. Write a paragraph describing what the right to the "pursuit of Happiness" provides for you.
2. Write a paragraph discussing how the right of liberty may be compromised in dire medical circumstances.
3. Write a paragraph describing how you may best fulfill the gift of the right to life.

Know What You Want

IT'S USEFUL TO BEAR IN mind that considering one's own death may be extraordinarily difficult. It may be stressful and upsetting to even think about such a possibility. No one wants to consider his own demise, and no one wants to imagine circumstances that would place her in such a situation. But we will proceed with courage and fortitude. We will forge ahead. So, first, you need to consider what living circumstances are acceptable. Do you wish to maintain life at any cost? For many, this is a self-evident proposition. Life itself is a primary good. For such persons, an advance directive is not needed. Medical science has the ability to prolong life as such far beyond what would occur if nature were left to take its course. For example, persons with terminal cancer can be kept alive for months or years by means of life-supporting treatment such as artificial nutrition, artificial hydration, and artificial ventilators. Also, the pain of cancer can be reduced by various opioid medications. Of course, without such intervention, the person's physiological life-support mechanisms would fail and he or she would die. From many points of view, these measures are good things. But many persons are kept alive by well-meaning families who are unable to let their loved ones go to their permanent rest and by physicians who believe their primary responsibility is to preserve life at whatever cost.

If you're a person for whom life-at-any-cost does not represent an acceptable outcome or is not a match for your philosophy of living, enacting an advance directive is part of your means for safeguarding your future. When preparing your advance directive, it's critical to know what you want. Additionally, it's important to emphasize that your preferences are not set in stone. You may revise the document at any time. The most important thing is to get your advance directive on paper, notarized, and distributed among your loved ones, friends, and trusted physicians.

You will be specifying your preferences and desires for a situation in which you are unable to make your wishes known. Various medical problems and accidents may render you unconscious or worse. Your advance directive is designed to protect you in the medical environment, where anything and often everything can happen. You will be choosing what sorts of procedures you will allow, and you will be specifying the life circumstances, that is, the quality of life, you deem acceptable or unacceptable.

In the worst scenarios, a person may suffer a serious brain injury that causes him to lose not only substantial functional ability, but also the capacity for decision-making. The most extreme case is a persistent vegetative state. In a persistent vegetative state, the person is awake but unaware of herself and her surroundings. The person may blink, swallow, and otherwise react to stimuli, but these are lower level reflexes only. None of these reflexive responses is indicative of higher brain functioning. The person's reflexes do not represent actions of a self-aware, interactive consciousness, but rather are mere demonstrations of physiological responses. Essentially the body is living, but the person is not conscious and has no ability to interact or respond meaningfully.

In a less extreme situation the person may regain consciousness following a stroke, but has lost the ability to understand others or to make herself understood. Such circumstances represent damage to regions of the brain known as Broca's area or Wernicke's area. The loss of ability to understand or express speech is termed aphasia. The ongoing challenge is for others to assess the likelihood of such a person regaining his ability to communicate. Aphasia may be permanent. From your current perspective of a person with full capacity, you may consider various potential scenarios and decide you would not wish to continue to live under such constraints. But in order for your surrogate to be able to make your preferences and desires known, your choices need to be specified in your advance directive.

Once you've been resuscitated via CPR and/or brought back to consciousness by means of various medical procedures, applying the specifications in your advance directive may be challenging if you have not been sufficiently precise. Your surrogate may personally find it very difficult to "pull the plug", that is, to insist on removal of life-sustaining therapy such as artificial nutrition and hydration. You can counter this natural reluctance in two ways. First, be as specific as possible in the section of your advance directive that identifies your preferences and wishes. For example, you could state, "If I have not regained my capacity for decision-making within 30 days and I continue to require artificial nutrition and hydration, I do not wish to continue living in such circumstances and request that all life-sustaining treatment including artificial nutrition and hydration be withdrawn." Additionally, you could state, "If I have not regained consciousness after 30 days, I do not wish to continue living in such circumstances and request that all life-sustaining treatment including artificial nutrition and hydration be withdrawn." Second, you must carefully select the person who will serve as your surrogate and you must discuss the content of your advance directive with that person, regardless of whether he or she is a family member or friend. In your discussion, you'll emphasize that your surrogate will be carrying out your wishes. Your surrogate will stand in for you and speak on your behalf, stating the choices you have specified in your advance directive. Importantly, you'll make it clear to your surrogate that he or she is not the one making the decision, for example, to remove life-supporting treatment. You are the one who has made that decision. Your surrogate will express your choices, in the event you are not able to do so.

The circumstances under which the provisions of an advance directive become applicable vary somewhat, depending on your state of residence. For example, the California Advance Care Directive Form (California Probate Code Section 4701) provides a "Choice Not to Prolong Life" checkbox. This choice would apply when (1) there is "an incurable or irreversible condition that will result in death within a relatively short time"; (2) you are unconsciousness, and there is a reasonable degree of medical certainty that consciousness will not be regained; or (3) "the likely risks and burdens of treatment would outweigh the expected benefits". The California Advance Care Directive Form also states "you may strike any wording you do not want". Thus, the conditions for implementing an advance directive are somewhat fluid and may be subject to interpretation by the ethics committee of the hospital in which you are a patient. You will assist all parties concerned in following your preferences for end-of-life care by ensuring that (1) your surrogate understands your precise wishes and (2) your instructions listed in your advance directive are as specific as possible. For example, your advance directive could state that in the case of prolonged loss of capacity (such as 90 days), you would consider that the risks and burdens of treatment would outweigh the expected benefits. In other words, your quality of life would not be acceptable and therefore the risks and burdens would be unacceptable. Such a statement may help fulfill the California requirements and substantiate your end-of-life care requests.

In another jurisdiction, the State of New Jersey Department of Health indicates that life-sustaining treatment (LST) may be withheld or withdrawn when you are permanently unconscious or in a terminal condition, when LST would only prolong an imminent death or would likely be ineffective, or when LST would likely be of more harm than benefit. Again, your advance directive statement, that in the case of prolonged loss of capacity you would consider that the risks and burdens of treatment would outweigh the expected benefits, may help fulfill State of New Jersey requirements for implementation of your end-of-life care requests. The preponderance of the California and New Jersey requirements for implementation of your advance directive requests may be fulfilled by specific statements. For example, you could state, "I wish life-sustaining treatment to be withheld or withdrawn if I have been deemed permanently unconscious or if my condition is terminal. I wish life-sustaining treatment to be withheld or withdrawn if such treatment would only prolong an imminent death or would likely be ineffective." Reiterating the language of your home state's requirements in your advance directive, and adding appropriate qualifiers, may assist the responsible parties, that is, your surrogate and hospital staff, in upholding your stated preferences and wishes.

Ultimately, in consideration of the potential finality of end-of-life decision-making, many more parties than yourself may be involved in your medical care. The U.S. Supreme Court has affirmed that "a competent person has a constitutionally protected liberty interest in refusing unwanted medical treatment" [*Cruzan v. Director, Missouri Department of Health*, 497 U.S. 261 (1990)], including a constitutionally protected right to refuse lifesaving nutrition and hydration. Thus, if you're conscious and have capacity to make medical decisions, you have the right to refuse treatment. When you have lost capacity, your advance directive and your surrogate represent the best means for having your wishes and preferences fulfilled.

Know What You Want: Going Further

Personal Reflection

Consider the possibility that the process of reflecting on one's death may represent a powerful affirmation of one's life. Sit quietly for 10 minutes and contemplate what it might be like to no longer have a physical existence, that is, to be dead as we most often use this term. Next, experience the contrast between these reflections and the actuality of being alive. What opens up for you?

Action Steps

1. Write a paragraph discussing the circumstances under which you would and would not wish to be resuscitated.
2. Write a paragraph discussing the circumstances under which you would and would not wish to receive artificial nutrition and artificial hydration.
3. Create a list of three specific statements you want to include in your advance directive regarding quality of life.
4. Write a paragraph describing the personal importance of these specifications in regard to acceptable and unacceptable quality of life.

Step 1: Plan Ahead

AN **ADVANCE DIRECTIVE** IS A legal document by which you can specify your personal preferences and desires regarding health care decision-making in circumstances in which you're not able to speak on your own behalf. It's very important that we understand this complex introductory statement. First, an advance directive provides a formal record of your wishes in situations requiring medical decision-making, in the case in which you, having previously had the cognitive capacity to make your preferences known, have lost such capacity, temporarily or permanently. However, if you haven't enacted a formal advance directive, your medical treatment is determined by the medical standards of your community. Typically, any and all available life-saving measures will be utilized when needed, based on the presumption that saving a life is always better than the alternative. This is probably not what many people would want, given the significant loss of quality of life that accompanies life-saving treatment following prolonged loss of consciousness associated with traumatic brain injury and heart attack. In many cases your life, as such, has been saved. But much of what we have always taken for granted, such as speaking, writing, reading, feeding ourselves, and generally taking care of ourselves, has been lost or substantially compromised. An advance directive helps to counter such eventualities by formalizing what you want and don't want done in a severe health care emergency.

The most important thing about an advance directive is having one. But in order to have an advance directive, of course, you must actually sit down and write it out. Preparation time will help a great deal. There are numerous official web sites that offer instructions on how to compose a suitable and appropriate advance directive. For example, the New York State Bar Association makes relevant forms freely available, including a New York Health Care Proxy Form (provided by the NYS Department of Health — http://www.nysba.org/Sections/Elder/MR_National_Healthcare_Decisions_D On the West Coast, California Probate Code Section 4701 enumerates a highly detailed, comprehensive Advance Health Care Directive form. This well-designed template contains a section for designating your agent (power of attorney for health care), specific statements regarding your agent's authority and when such authority becomes effective, and several sections regarding instructions for health care, such as end-of-life decisions. As another example, an editable State of West Virginia living will is found here.

Other important resources include community groups and church/synagogue groups. Senior citizen activist groups such as AARP provide assistance in composing an advance directive that will meet your needs. For example, Advance Directives: Creating a Living Will and Health Care Power of Attorney, on the AARP site, provides valuable definitions for key concepts and several useful links, including a page where you can download state-specific advance directive forms. The main point is to spend a few hours, over the course of two or three days, researching what's available and what your choices are. Then, having done your due diligence, you're ready to sit down and write your advance directive.

Most of the advance directive templates include a section labeled "other wishes" or "optional" where you can specify, in your own words, your desires and preferences. It's critically important to be as specific as possible. Merely saying, "I want to die in peace", is far from sufficient. Most hospital staff will interpret this in their own way, and their understanding of "dying in peace" may vastly differ from your intentions. For example, you may not want to be kept alive in unacceptable circumstances, but what is actually happening is you're being fed pain-killing medication to dull your senses and keep you "peaceful".

The two main components of your specifications or orders are the things you want to avoid having done to you and the quality of life that you will find acceptable. Again, writing an advance directive is very challenging. It may be upsetting to think about types of medical treatment and their consequences, or to consider which compromises to quality of life we would deem acceptable, especially as we're accustomed to being healthy and well. For most of us, we will continue to be healthy. But stuff happens, and we need to be prepared. If you fail to plan, of course, you plan to fail.

Medical treatments that will likely be of concern and about which you may want to specify special instructions include cardiopulmonary resuscitation (CPR), artificial nutrition and hydration, artificial respiration, surgical procedures, and dialysis. Importantly, you need to be as precise as possible when communicating your wishes and preferences. You could state, "Do not resuscitate me if the amount of time I've been unconscious is unknown or greater than four minutes." You could specify, "If more than 30 days have passed, I have not regained my ability to feed myself, and I am unable to communicate my preferences or desires via speech, writing, or other method, then I want any and all life-saving measures, such as artificial nutrition/hydration/ventilation, to be discontinued." Then, be as clear as possible about the quality of life you do find acceptable. You could state, "I don't want to live like Karen Quinlan, Nancy Cruzan, or Terri Schiavo. In other words, I don't want to live for longer than 30 days in a persistent vegetative state. I don't want to live if I am unable to communicate or have lost the mental capacity to think for myself. I don't want to live if I can't meaningfully read a book or watch TV. I don't want to be dependent on others for the maintenance of my physical functioning." Specifying the quality of life that is acceptable to you will help others, that is, your family, your friends, and hospital staff, understand your intentions and help them to uphold your wishes and desires.

The Bottom Line

Despite all your best efforts, hospital staff may be reluctant to implement your preferences and desires regarding medical decision-making. It's important to recognize that implementing a decision to terminate life support is not made by one staff member on his or her own. For example, the attending physician on the day shift may support such a course of action, but the night shift attending physician does not. Or the hospital ethicist is in favor of upholding your instructions in your advance directive, but members of the nursing staff believe another month of watchful waiting is appropriate. Hospital administrators may be concerned with adverse publicity. Hospital legal advisors may recommend caution in the face of resistance by family members not named as your surrogate. Most hospitals have created institution-wide ethics committees to manage their approach to such important issues. Committee membership typically includes representatives from the major hospital medical departments, the nursing department, and the social work department; hospital administrators; the hospital ethicist; and community clergy and other interested citizens. Ultimately, your advance directive's clarity and specificity will help all concerned parties reach the conclusions that you wish them to reach regarding your medical care.

It's never too soon to write your advance directive. Such a document is not only for those who are over age 65. As age 60 more and more becomes the new 40, advance directives become ever more important. Should a teenager have an advance directive? This is probably not realistic, but young people who are older than age 20 should certainly have one. Each of the three signature court cases in this arena, concerning Karen Quinlan, Nancy Cruzan, and Terri Schiavo, involved women in their 20s. The unexpected happens and it's very important to be prepared. It was not sufficient for Terri Schiavo to have told her husband and close friends that she would not want to "live like that", that is, in a persistent vegetative state. In order to ensure, as much as is reasonably possible, that your wishes and preferences are followed, you not only need to tell family and friends about your preferences. You need to have an advance directive.

In today's world we need to protect ourselves against unwanted use of medical technology. Physicians practice medicine defensively and we, as patients, need to help them to act appropriately on our behalf. A strong, clearly worded advance directive, backed by testimony of friends and loved ones, will help ensure that your wishes will be honored.

Importantly, in addition to writing your advance directive, you should specify the person who is legally empowered to make medical decisions on your behalf. Such a person, known as a surrogate, agent, or health care proxy, is named in a Health Care Proxy document. A Health Care Proxy Form provided by New York State is found here. Instructions for filling out the Health Care Proxy Form are found here. In California, Part 1 of the Advance Health Care Directive is a Power of Attorney for Health Care. An editable State of West Virginia Medical Power of Attorney form is found here.

The person you name via power of attorney is your surrogate or agent, the person authorized by you to make medical decisions on your behalf if you have become unable to do so. Both California and New York specify that your health care proxy or surrogate has the power to direct the provision, withholding, or withdrawal of artificial hydration and artificial nutrition, as well as use of or withholding of cardiopulmonary resuscitation. You may provide your agent with as much authority as you wish.

Once your advance directive documents are completed you may, in some jurisdictions, register these legal papers with a state agency. California, for example, maintains the Advance Health Care Directive Registry. The State of California Registration of Written Advance Health Care Directive is found here. The Vermont Advance Directive Registry is found here.

Additional steps to take include distributing copies of your advance directive and health care proxy form to your proxy or surrogate, close family members, your family physician, and your attorney. You should carry a card in your wallet specifying the location of your advance directive documents. Make sure you instruct your family physician to include a copy of your advance directive in your medical record.

Step 1: Going Further

Personal Reflection

You're never too young or too old to write your advance directive. Sit quietly for a few minutes and consider what it would be like to to lose your cognitive ability to make decisions. Next, consider that once you've lost such ability it's too late to make plans to compensate for your loss. Spend a few minutes thinking about the peace of mind you'd obtain by preparing for such an eventuality, and what such preparation might mean for you and your loved ones.

Action Steps

1. To begin the process of writing your advance directive, read a sample Health Care Proxy form.
2. Next, create a list of five persons who might serve as your **health care proxy** or **surrogate**.
3. Create a master list of the name, address, and contact information for one of two close family members or friends, your family physician, religious adviser (if applicable), and attorney or accountant.

Step 2: Write It Down

ALL WRITERS KNOW THAT HAVING a good idea in your head is not sufficient for the task at hand. What's required after the good idea arrives is sitting down and actually committing text to paper. It's the application of your fingers to the keyboard (or for traditionalists, pen to paper) that will create a real article, book, or screenplay. You have to get the words onto the page. The work begins when you start writing.

Of course, preparation counts for a great deal. You do research, you read articles, you listen to talks on YouTube, and your subconscious gets into motion. In *Psycho-Cybernetics* (1960), Maxwell Maltz, M.D., described the subconscious as a goal-achieving machine, a built-in guidance system that directs your actions toward fulfillment of specific goals. In his groundbreaking book Maltz wrote, "Your built-in servo-mechanism functions both as a 'guidance system' to automatically steer you in the right direction to achieve certain goals . . . and also as an 'electronic brain' which can function automatically to solve problems." Your subconscious is always at work seeking opportunities by means of which you may fulfill your intentions. But you need to specify your goals and give precise instructions to your subconscious. By providing definite directions such as "I want to live in a 3000-square-foot home on a half-acre of land one-quarter mile from the beach", you are priming the pump of your built-in guidance system. A seemingly magical process ensues in which your subconscious looks at your project from all angles and then makes choices — unknown to your conscious mind — from among the myriad facts, circumstances, situations, and people presented to your experience every moment. Your subconscious then steers you toward making choices that will be best for you in terms of fulfilling your specific goals. Your subconscious helps smooth your path toward your objective and helps you achieve your goal. (The term *cybernetics* is derived from *kybernetikos*, the ancient Greek word meaning "good at steering", referring to the skills of a helmsman.)

The mundane yet important task of finding a convenient parking space is an elementary example of how your built-in guidance system works. Those who consistently find a good parking spot even in heavily trafficked downtown areas and busy shopping malls will immediately recognize this process, even if they've never intentionally consulted their built-in parking-spot-seeking mechanism. Another example is meeting, seemingly randomly, a previously unknown person who becomes your business partner or is otherwise crucial to your success in your chosen field. Your subconscious is on the job, regardless of your knowledge of such a process, provided your intention (desire) is clear.

This digression focusing on psycho-cybernetics highlights the importance of intentionality and preparation in fulfilling your aims and plans. Once you've made the commitment to designing and writing your advance directive, your subconscious will begin to search for and present to your conscious mind materials that will be of assistance in composing your document. For example, a May 2014 article in a special *New York Times* "Retirement" section focused on advance directives and end-of-life planning.

Once you've given thought to these highly personal matters and possibly discussed your concerns with family members or close friends, you're ready to sit down and write. The most important component of your advance directive is your specific instructions regarding what you want done and what you don't want done, as well as your detailed directives regarding acceptable quality of life. For example, regarding resuscitation, you might simply state, "In the event that my heart has stopped and I have stopped breathing, do not resuscitate me." (If this is your preference, you could carry a DNR (do-not-resuscitate) card in your wallet, to ensure that well-meaning good samaritans or emergency responders do not, in fact, resuscitate you.) Regarding use of life-sustaining treatment, you could state, "If I am unable to speak, write, read, or otherwise communicate effectively, and these circumstances have persisted for a consecutive period of 30 days, prolongation of my life by means of life-sustaining treatment is not acceptable to me. In such circumstances, the harms of such treatment will outweigh the presumed benefits, and I insist that life-sustaining treatment be withdrawn." Becoming familiar with the <u>advance directive regulations in your state of residence</u> will assist you in designing additional specific instructions regarding your medical care in circumstances in which you have lost the capacity to make your own decisions.

You may want to share your advance directive with family and friends and request their feedback and input. Such a process will provide you and your loved ones a chance to reflect on the best choices in dire circumstances, that is, what is most right for you and how you want things to go if you are approaching the end of your life on earth.

Once you've designed and written your advance directive, the next step is to give copies of this document to a few select family members and/or close friends. You may have a copy notarized and keep this copy in a designated location at home. Make sure to tell your spouse or partner, a close friend, and/or your surrogate where your advance directive is stored. Give a copy to your primary care physician and instruct your doctor to include your advance directive in your medical record. Instruct a loved one and/or your surrogate to ensure that your advance directive and/or DNR order is included in your medical record, in the case in which you require hospitalization. Also, if you are hospitalized, it is your surrogate's responsibility to make sure the attending physician and nursing staff know about your preferences. The need for these action steps should be addressed with your surrogate at the time he or she agrees to take on that role. Your surrogate should speak with the hospital ethicist, too, to make sure everyone is informed and on board. There is strength in numbers. Such action steps help ensure that a good outcome will be obtained, that is, your preferences and wishes will be honored.

Your advance directive should be clear, concise, and consistent. Also, be sure to revisit your advance directive and review your specific instructions every two years or so. Your preferences and wishes may change over time. For example, your perspective on these matters at age 60 may differ from your views at age 50. The more up-to-date an advance directive, the more likely it is to be upheld. Protect yourself and your family by taking these measures on your own behalf.

Step 2: Going Further

Personal Reflection

Consider the optimal circumstances under which you'd complete your sojourn on this planet. If you had the opportunity to choose, what would they be? Many people would choose to die peacefully while they were asleep. Others might imagine going out in a personal blaze of glory, whatever that might be. Now consider the value of life itself. Of course, most of us have never really thought about life in this way, so this might take some practice. Think about what "quality of life" means to you and whether loss of acceptable quality of life is sufficient grounds for requesting the withholding or withdrawal of life-sustaining treatment.

Action Steps

1. Using the various templates referenced in Step 1: Plan Ahead, write the first draft of your advance directive.
2. Write a paragraph describing what having your own advance directive means to you and what it might mean for your family.
3. Read Ode: Intimations of Immortality from Recollections of Early Childhood by William Wordsworth and Ode to a Nightingale by John Keats. Write a paragraph describing what insights and inspiration, if any, you've gained from these literary classics and what's opened up for you as a result of your reading.

Step 3: Whom Do You Trust?

"WHO DO YOU TRUST?" WAS the ungrammatical but tremendously popular 1950s–1960s television game show that launched the career of Johnny Carson. "Who [really, whom] do you trust?" becomes critically important when choosing the person you will designate as your surrogate. Your surrogate is that individual who will assert your rights and interests in the area of health care decision-making, if you have become unable to speak on your own behalf. In other words, your surrogate is the living embodiment of the judgments or choices you would make if you were able to do so. Your surrogate will execute the terms of your advance directive, provided you have had the wisdom and foresight to have made one.

Your surrogate will be required to make life-or-death decisions for you. If you've decided you don't want a feeding tube stuck in your gut (artificial nutrition and hydration) when you're not capable of eating and drinking on your own, or if you have a terminal illness and don't want to be resuscitated in case of a cardiac event, your surrogate will be the one protecting your wishes and preferences. In case the worst happens, your surrogate will speak for you, protecting your right to live your life the way you want to live it and protecting your right to die if the circumstances dictate such a possibility.

The conditions under which your surrogate will be called to fulfill his or her duty will be very challenging. The surrogate may find herself at the center of dire circumstances in which a good friend or loved one is faced with death. At such a critical juncture, objectivity is a most important and precious quality. Your surrogate is charged with asserting and upholding your preferences and desires, rather than his own wants and needs or understandably selfish desire to keep you alive, to not let you die. Thoughtful, well-considered decision-making is required. A surrogate may feel guilty. A surrogate may feel as if he can't make the decision. She may secretly wish someone else had the responsibility. Therefore, it's important to choose a person whom you can trust to get the job done. This requires at least one face-to-face conversation in which you inform your surrogate about your specific preferences regarding end-of-life circumstances. For example, you might state that if you're found unconscious and a medical examination shows you've had a stroke, then you do not want to be resuscitated. Or you might inform your surrogate that if you've suffered a traumatic brain injury (for example, subsequent to a car crash) and after 60 days you still cannot speak, write, or read, then you do not wish to remain on life-supporting measures such as a feeding tube and/or mechanical ventilation (artificial breathing).

None of this is easy, not for you and not for the person who is agreeing to be your surrogate. You must specify your preferences, in as much detail as is reasonably possible. Doing so will enable your surrogate to speak effectively on your behalf. In contrast, if you've only stated, "I don't want to live like a vegetable", such a generalization is open to wide interpretation and your surrogate's mission to represent your interests will be severely compromised. Thus, being specific in your advance directive helps avoid a bad outcome, such as your being kept alive in circumstances that do not fulfill your requirements for acceptable quality of life.

Of course, you substantially help your surrogate by creating, signing, and notarizing an advance directive. The presence of such a formal document legitimizes your surrogate's assertions regarding your preferences and desires. However, regardless of the presence of your advance directive, your surrogate may experience feelings of guilt and suffer a crisis of conscience when confronted with the responsibility of recommending actions that will result in your demise.

Such guilt and indecision arise from confusion on the part of the surrogate regarding his actual function. In your conversations with your surrogate, you must remind her that she is not the one making the decision. Although she may speak the words, "Remove the artificial nutrition and hydration", the decision to state that demand is not hers. As your surrogate, she is merely carrying out your specific choices. She is not expressing her personal choice. Rather, she is fulfilling your definite demand. In legal terms, this process is referred to as "substituted judgment". The *substituted judgment standard* requires surrogate decision making to be based on the incapacitated patient's known preferences and values. [Buchanan AE, Brock DW: Deciding for Others: The Ethics of Surrogate Decision Making. New York, NY, Cambridge University Press, 1989] The surrogate applies those preferences and values to the patient's condition and prognosis, and takes action based on a match between the clinical circumstances and your expressly stated wishes and desires. The surrogate can be relieved of any burden of guilt, as she is solely fulfilling your requests. It is not her choice or decision that she is expressing. It is yours.

Regarding the selection of an appropriate surrogate, it may seem that a family member is the right choice. After all, you may think that it is a family member who best knows you. But it may be wisest to vest such decisions in a person who does not have family ties. By selecting a friend rather than a spouse, sibling, or child as your surrogate, you eliminate family bonds and considerations that may cause the surrogate to want to keep you alive, regardless of the quality of life you will experience and have previously rejected in your advance directive and prior conversations with your surrogate.

Being confronted with a severely ill or dying spouse, sibling, or parent could potentially be overwhelming. Unresolved issues and concerns immediately and unintentionally are retrieved from memory and bubble to the surface. It may become very difficult for your surrogate to remain objective. Further, family disputes may arise, despite the designation of one family member as the surrogate. For example, an adult child may strongly advocate for erring on the side of caution, insisting that all life-sustaining measures be maintained. The patient's sister or brother, the aunt or uncle of that child, argues equally strongly for upholding the patient's wishes to not continue to live at a reduced level of quality of life. A friend or business associate, rather than a family member, may be immune from such considerations and able to more effectively represent your preferences. Such a person may be able to appropriately render a substituted judgment on your behalf.

Substituted Judgment vs. Best Interests

Standard

In **substituted judgment**, your surrogate attempts to establish what decisions you would have made if you were competent to make a decision. These conclusions can be based on your desires and preferences expressed in previous verbal statements or the surrogate's knowledge of your beliefs and values. In the best case, the surrogate bases her or his judgment on the preferences and desires you have expressly stated in your advance directive. Your surrogate will "substitute" your judgment regarding the clinical circumstances and medical decision-making required by those circumstances. If no advance directive exists and your preferences and desires have not been expressed to family or friends, the **best interests standard** is utilized. Hospital staff, supported by input from the hospital ethicist and the patient's close relatives and/or close friends, will make medical decisions based on your best interests, that is, based on the most likely best medical outcome. The basis for a best interest decision is what a reasonable person would choose after considering all the options and alternatives. Optimally, you have created an advance directive and designated a surrogate (health care proxy). Your surrogate will utilize substituted judgement, if such dire circumstances arise.

The choice of a surrogate should be a deliberate decision. Your surrogate is a person you can literally trust with your life. Such a choice requires you to be objective and not be swayed by your own emotional considerations, such as "Will my spouse or child be offended or hurt if I don't choose him for this important responsibility?" Your main concern is to choose a person who is most likely to speak accurately on your behalf, one who will authentically state your preferences. Such a person will best be able to be your surrogate when you most need such an advocate and representative.

Step 3: Going Further

Personal Reflection

Consider what you're asking your surrogate to accomplish on your behalf. How would you feel and what might you go through, if you were the surrogate and required by your commitment to request withholding or withdrawal of life-sustaining treatment for your friend or family member. Now, consider who among your family and friends is best suited to fulfill such a role.

Action Steps

1. Review the list of potential surrogates you created in <u>Step 1: Plan Ahead</u>.
2. Based on your instincts, reflections, and best judgment, choose the individual whom you will request to be your surrogate.
3. Make a new list of topics and concerns you want to discuss with your potential surrogate. What do you want him or her to know regarding your plans and intentions? How can you best support your surrogate and how can your surrogate best support you?

Step 4: Phone a Friend

ONCE YOU'VE WRITTEN YOUR ADVANCE directive, it's very important to tell people about it. To borrow a line from the well-known TV game show, *Who Wants To Be a Millionaire*, you need to "phone a friend". Call family members and close friends to let them know you've created this important document. You should tell several people or more about the steps you've taken to protect your future and your family's future. Tell those you're calling why you're including them among the people you've chosen to receive this important communication. Next, ask them if it's OK to talk about such personal matters. If it is, then let them know what's important to you regarding the circumstances in which an advance directive may be required. You want to tell your loved ones, close family members, and close friends about your wishes and preferences in potentially dire medical circumstances.

Share with those close to you the specific details of your advance directive regarding cardiopulmonary resuscitation and life-sustaining treatments. Such a conversation may seem unnecessarily alarming, morbid, or bizarre, but tell them why you want to discuss such concerns. Tell them a bit about what you've learned regarding the unwanted prolongation of the lives of Karen Ann Quinlan, Nancy Cruzan, and Terri Schiavo. Let your family and friends know you don't want to live like that, referencing your specific preferences and desires. By having this conversation you're enlisting their support in case the worst happens to you. Let them know you may need their assistance at some future date. Tell those close to you that you will be identifying a surrogate in your advance directive, and explain that a surrogate is the person who will speak on your behalf in case you're unable to do so. By means of these conversations, you may be able to determine who among your family and friends would best be able to fulfill the duties and responsibilities of your surrogate.

As discussed in <u>Step 3: Whom Do You Trust?</u>, your surrogate is the person who will express your wishes and preferences as delineated in your advance directive. Importantly, your surrogate must understand and be clear that he or she will be stating *your* preferences and desires regarding choice of medical procedures, rather than what they think should or should not be done. Effectively, your surrogate will function, if needed, as your mouthpiece. It is your surrogate's responsibility to make sure that your choices, most likely regarding withholding or withdrawing life-sustaining treatment, will be expressed and upheld. "Phoning a friend", in whatever form this takes, whether an actual call or meeting for coffee or a meal, will assist you in choosing the family member or friend with the appropriate qualities of trustworthiness, steadfastness, and strength of character. You will select the person whom you believe can be counted on in the direst of circumstances, that is, the possible end of your life.

But there's no need for doom and gloom. Although the content of these conversations is serious, it is empowering to be light and upbeat. After all, ultimately, we will all be faced with our demise. Our purpose is to make sure that we are the ones who are in control of the medical process, if there is one, at the end of life. Remind your family and friends that you're not asking them to "pull the plug". You're asking them to be able to testify on your behalf (figuratively or literally, if needed), to be able to say, "Yes, this is what he or she wanted to have done. He or she called me and told me about it and we discussed these matters in detail." In a very real sense you're asking a select group of people to stand up for you, if needed, and affirm the types of medical treatment you have stated you wish to receive in potentially severe or terminal circumstances. You're asking for the support of your friends and family in helping you live your life the way you desire to live it, that is, being able to choose an acceptable quality of life or declining to continue living if faced with unacceptable circumstances.

A few professional people should be informed, as well. Your family physician, the leader of your religious community, and your attorney should all be apprised of the details of your advance directive. If the worst happens, these professionals will be able to come forward and confirm your wishes and preferences regarding quality of life and end-of-life decision-making. Also, make sure your doctor includes your advance directive in your medical chart in his or her office. Insist that she or he place a copy of your advance directive in your hospital chart, in the case in which you're brought to the hospital but are unable to effectively communicate your choices regarding medical decision-making.

If the worst happens and your well-being and possibly your life are on the line, but you're unable to speak for yourself, medical decisions will be made by hospital personnel. Many people will be looking at your chart including various attending physicians, your primary care doctor, and nursing staff. Regarding the actual implementation of your advance directive, policies vary among hospitals. The hospital ethicist as well as hospital administrators may become involved. The ethicist will likely participate in any decision to withhold or withdraw life-sustaining treatment. Depending on the institution, the hospital ethics committee may have the responsibility for such decision-making. The support of your family, friends, and selected professionals will assist the hospital ethicist and/or ethics committee in comprehending and acknowledging the appropriateness of your advance directive specifications. Your family and friends will help the hospital staff to come to the appropriate decisions on your behalf. There may be some snags and delays, but owing to your foresight in lining up in advance people who will support you, you have helped yourself to secure the best possible outcome. The strong team you have put together, in addition to your detailed advance preparation, that is, your advance directive, will greatly facilitate your wishes and preferences being honored and upheld.

Build a Strong Community
Your interactions and conversations with your friends and family may have another important benefit. Those close to you may be inspired to take similar actions on their own behalf. In fact, you may be called on to support their process of creating an advance directive. Altogether, a stronger community is created in which people gain enhanced certainty, personal and financial security, and peace of mind regarding what may happen to them, in the future, regarding medical care at the end of life.

Step 4: Going Further

Personal Reflection

Consider how it might be possible to be upbeat in a conversation regarding end-of-life decision-making. Not by being inauthentic, of course, but rather by coming from a place of gratitude, both for the goodness of your own life and the generosity of your family member or friend in being willing to assist you if needed. Consider your relationship with that person and all your shared experiences. How might you support your surrogate in potentially doing what you're asking him or her to do?

Action Steps

1. Phone or meet with the family member or friend you believe best capable of serving as your surrogate, and invite her or him to take on this role.. Discuss the details of your advance directive, explain what may be required of your surrogate, and to the best of your ability, answer their questions and address their concerns.

2. Be sure to emphasize that your surrogate will be speaking for you, in the case in which you cannot speak for yourself. It is not the surrogate's role to make the decision he or she thinks is right. Your surrogate's responsibility is to make your wishes, preferences, and desires known and to request action that you would want taken. Essentially, your surrogate is your mouthpiece and will express your (substituted) judgment, in the case in which you cannot do so for yourself. Discuss

these matters with your surrogate and ensure he or she fully comprehends what may be needed and that you're in agreement.

3. Read Shakespeare's <u>Sonnet LX</u> and <u>Sonnet LXIV</u>. Write a paragraph describing your responses to these poems.

Step 5: Keep It Simple!

YOUR ADVANCE DIRECTIVE SHOULD BE as clear and straightforward as possible. It's important to be specific regarding a few well-chosen scenarios, that is, the most likely situations that might occur following a medical emergency or in the case of terminal illness. But attempting to cover all bases will make it very difficult for hospital staff and even your surrogate to determine what it is you are actually intending. You can't account for every possibility and attempting to do so will detract substantially from the purpose of your advance directive, which is to ensure that your desires and preferences be upheld regarding medical care at the end-of-life.

Two key areas of concern are

- Use of cardiopulmonary resuscitation (CPR)
- Use of life-sustaining treatment such as artificial nutrition, artificial hydration, and artificial ventilation

You should include specific instructions regarding both sets of circumstances. The main concern with CPR is the possibility of being revived after more than four minutes of heart failure. Brain cells begin to die after being deprived of oxygen for approximately four minutes. If you're discovered without a heartbeat and the the time you've been unconscious is unknown, then it is likely that if you are revived you will have lost some or much of your higher brain function. You could state in your advance directive that in such a scenario, you do not wish to be resuscitated. Regarding life-sustaining treatment, presuming you've been revived from an unconscious state and have lost higher brain function, you could state you wish such treatment to be withdrawn if you have not regained the ability to communicate within 60 days, for example. Essentially, you don't want people to have to make guesses for you. Vague statements or overly complex instructions will cause hospital staff to resort to their default process, which is to save lives. They will do whatever it takes to save your life if you haven't provided clear, specific orders regarding alternate measures.

For emphasis, you could state that quality of life is of utmost importance to you. You could state, "Do not resuscitate me if I have been unconscious for an unknown period of time." Additionally, you may state, "I do not wish to be kept alive by artificial methods in excess of 60 consecutive days." Basically, you're stating (if this is your preference) that you do not wish to be kept alive if you've lost cognitive ability and can't do things for yourself. If your body recovers and continues functioning after all the machines and tubes have been withdrawn, so be it. But you desire the opportunity for your physiological systems to fail, if that is what's going to happen.

Importantly, you'll specify the person who will serve as your surrogate, the individual you are authorizing to make health care decisions on your behalf in the case in which you are unable to do so. The State of California, for example, terms such a person your agent. You specify your agent in a Power of Attorney for Health Care (included in the California Advance Health Care Directive form). This power of attorney becomes effective "when your primary doctor determines that you lack the ability to understand the nature and consequences of your health care decisions or the ability to make and communicate your health care decisions". New York State terms this person your Health Care Proxy or "health care agent". Be sure to avoid choosing your surrogate based on sentiment. The best surrogate is one who is tough-minded, one who will persist in her or his mission to fulfill your wishes and preferences in potentially dire medical circumstances.

We can see that "keeping it simple" does not imply overlooking necessary steps or processes. Some time and effort is required to craft an appropriate and meaningful advance directive that clearly expresses your preferences and desires. You'll need to consider carefully what's most important to you. As you proceed, you may find yourself clarifying your values and gaining a deeper appreciation for the gift of life. You may discover that you no longer take each day for granted, but rather have begun to express gratitude for each additional day of life.

Finally, get some feedback from friends and family. If your loved ones and close acquaintances were going to take action on your behalf, what would they conclude from your advance directive? Would they know how to proceed? What loopholes or vague notions do they uncover in the imagined scenario of interpreting your stated wishes and preferences? Your advance directive is not a thesis or dissertation, but your language still needs to be clear and precise. Rewrite your advance directive, as needed, and resubmit it to your "reviewers". When you're satisfied that you've clearly expressed what you want done, sign and notarize your advance directive and distribute copies to appropriate persons, including your surrogate and family physician. Make sure to revisit and update your advance directive every few years.

Now, resolve to eat a healthy diet, exercise regularly, obtain sufficient rest, and get ready for the rest of your life!

Step 5: Going Further

Personal Reflection

Writing your advance directive helps prepare you and your family for dire medical scenarios. Now, consider the action steps you could take to improve your overall quality of health and minimize the likelihood of such circumstances. Recent scientific research has critically identified diet and lifestyle as key determinants of chronic disease such as cancer, heart disease, diabetes, and obesity. Primary lifestyle upgrades include regular, vigorous physical activity; a healthy diet; and sufficient rest. What would be required for you to begin to take such actions on your own behalf?

Action Steps

1. Make a list of five areas in which you could enhance your health and well-being. Be as specific as possible.
2. Now make a second list. For each item on your first list, identify two action steps to address each area of concern. Again, be as specific as possible. What you are doing, in effect, is creating a personalized lifestyle upgrade program.
3. Begin your program, consulting with your family physician as needed. You could, for example, set yourself a goal of following your program for 8, 10, or 12 weeks. Evaluate your progress at the end of the defined period, assess what you've accomplished, and set new goals for the next 8, 10, or 12 weeks. Be accountable to yourself, do the things you say

you're going to do, keep going, and be sure to celebrate your progress along the road to good health.

4. Although, in general, everyone knows the importance of instituting and maintaining healthy lifestyles, additional information may be of value. <u>Prevention of Chronic Disease by Means of Diet and Lifestyle Changes</u> is a highly detailed book chapter focusing on the developing world, but whose insights and recommendations are fully applicable to those living in developed nations.